Transition And Recovery

An SME Roadmap for Effective Strategy

By Cherry-Ann Carmelia Craigwell

About the Author

Cherry-Ann Craigwell is a consultant on commerce and business development. She has 27 years experience in Customer Service, Business and Process Development, Strategic Management and Business Culture Management. Her experience has shown there is the need for Small and Medium Enterprises to adopt fundamental practices to support their sustainability and competitiveness in the environment. Her passion for building business has purposed her to provide operational and strategy coaching services to Sole Traders and Small and Medium Sized Enterprises.

Other books written by the author –

> The Building Ideas Guide Handbook
>
> Utility Solutions for Businesses – USB for Small and Medium Enterprises

Transition and Recovery – An SME Roadmap for Effective Strategy Copyright © 2021 by Cherry-Ann Carmelia Craigwell. All rights reserved. Printed in the United States of America. No part of this book may be reproduced in any manner whatsoever without permission except in the case of brief quotation embodied in critical articles and reviews.

ISBN 9798450676296

Table of Contents

Introduction 6
Knowing Purpose 7
Navigating the Terrain 8
Small and Medium Enterprises Advantages 9
SME Classification 11
Understanding Strategy 13
Operational Strategy 14
Transformational Strategy 15
Strategy and Size 16
Business Life Stages 18
Transitions of the business 20
    Trust 20
    Self Sufficiency 20
    Innovation & Action 21
    Enterprising 21
    Distinction 22
    Cohesiveness 22
    Commitment 23
    Continuity 23
Change is Constant 24
    Change in Governance 25

- Additional Product / Service 25
- Additional Target Market 25
- Transformational Strategy Components 26
  - Have a Goal 26
  - A Developed Plan 26
  - Executing Team 27
  - Monitoring and Accountability 27
  - Process to Institutionalize 27
- Types of Transformational Strategies 28
  - Start Up Strategy 28
  - Diversification 28
  - Entering New Markets 28
  - Franchising 29
  - White Label Manufacturing / Sub Contracting 29
  - Acquisitions 29
  - Mergers 30
  - Exit Plan 30
- Business Recovery 31
- Types of Disasters 33
- Business Impact Analysis 36
- Business Continuity Plan 37
- Assets & Resources – Protection and Recovery 38

Finance 38

Furniture & Fixtures 39

Human Capital 39

Institution Knowledge 40

Inventory 40

Plant & Machinery 41

Property 41

Raw Materials 41

Vehicles 42

Opportunity in the Crisis 43

Conclusion 46

Introduction

A business owner is a capitalist; that is, you own the resources and the means of production for a product or a service. You are the first and most important investor in your business. It is important that you develop and implement strategies that will protect your investment and support the success of your business that will make it sustainable.

Every business based on its' classification, type and size will need to select the right target market, product or service, resource management support and financial strategies, to achieve an objective of stability and growth.

Transitioning and Recovery, however, are natural processes of growth and renewal for any business and it will become necessary for the business to adopt the right thoughts and accountable actions, to ensure that sustainability and growth of the business is achieved.

Knowing Purpose

Knowing and understanding the purpose of setting about on the journey of having your own business, is instrumental to the success of your business venture.

A person who is fatigued from working for others, who needs a side hustle or is technically skilled, will find any opportunity enticing to manage their own income flow, but that literally leaves you in a sea of opportunities without a specific destination.

This is different to a person who sees a need in the market and wants to provide a service or product that satisfies that need.

The destinations for both scenarios are different:

- One is to change a financial situation
- The other is to provide a service/product that is needed.

I selected these two scenarios as they are the most common reasons why someone will initiate a business venture.

It is important to understand purpose as it will guide the business in making key decisions.

Navigating the Terrain

We identified your purpose in establishing your business let's see what the terrain is like for an SME:

- It is averaged that 20% of start-ups fail within the first year.
- In the second year of business, it is expected of the remaining 80%, 34% will fail in their operations.
- Just over 50% of the remaining 53% will last till their fifth year.
- An average of 25% of the remaining 27% will celebrate the milestone of 15 years.

These statistics reflect that of 100 businesses started 7 will reach a 15 year milestone.

Most SME's fail because of:

- Limited strategy implementation
- Lack of accountability in operations
- No financial planning
- Blanket marketing
- Missing the GAPS in the market
- Limited network connectivity.

This is the roadmap some SMEs choose to travel.

Small and Medium Enterprises Advantages

Knowing where your business has an advantage is a good place to start to create or continue a successful journey.

The following lists the advantages SME's have in a market. Identify which of the following you can ascribe to your business's strengths:

- Delivery of products and services can be personalized.
- The ability to create passive income and capital reserves.
- Can easily adapt to environment changes through creativity.
- Better controls on product life cycle management.
- Creating market advantage by enhancing market relationship is easy.
- Ability to easily develop and control internal communication systems.
- Developing and maintaining desired culture in the business is manageable.
- Implementation of processes and policies tend to be uncomplicated and effortless.

Selecting a good roadmap and ensuring the business is employing strategy, operation efficiency, good financial planning and excellent marketing tools while leveraging on your identified strengths a business can improve on its competitiveness and sustainability.

This consistency in thought will assist the business in implementing easy transition strategies in the business's life stages, allowing a successful journey and longevity. It also gives coverage and support to survive some of the harshest situations your business may experience when there are sudden negative effects in the environment example; national disaster, change in industry elements or increase competition in the market.

SME Classification

The SME Model has three major classifications. These classifications are derived from the size of the SME.

Micro enterprise is a business that usually has not more than 50 employees. This business is either: a sole trader, partnership or a family limited liability. This business structure favors personal services, small retail outlets, entertainment, local consumption agriculture, niche products, small fast food places and light manufacturing.

Small Enterprises are businesses that will usually have less than 250 employees. These businesses are usually family operated, cooperatives, or limited liabilities. They best offer services to larger markets and provide commodity type products and services; like fast moving consumer goods. They favor services in technology, light manufacturing, export agriculture, finance, entertainment, retail outlets and large fast food chains.

Medium Enterprises are businesses that are limited liabilities or cooperatives. Their compliment of employees will average about 500 persons. These businesses can still be family owned but will be governed by a chairman and a board. As a medium enterprise the opportunities of a larger market can exist in the form of exporting products and services.

This business favors large manufacturing of niche products for export, commodity products, technology and finance.

Target markets and products and services must be determined on the ability to supply. This will guide you the business owner / manager to the right target market and whether the product /service is a commodity or should be specialized for a niche (more manageable and responsive) market. This is to ensure that the business can comfortably supply the market with a product it needs while using its resources effectively.

Understanding the size of the business and adopting the right strategy for your target market will be addressed in the chapter Strategy and Size.

Understanding Strategy

"Strategy is analytical thinking, progressive planning and accountable actions."

Cherry-Ann Craigwell

Your first strategy is the thoughts you have, of developing the opportunity of owning your business and engaging the discipline of putting together the resources to make it successful.

You are the first investor in your business, as such you are the initial capitalist in the venture and the resources of your time, expertise, finance, labor, physical assets and network are to be ***utilized effectively*** to bring about a profit.

The "***utilized effectively***" is the strategy. How that strategy is engaged determines the success of the business.

A business functions on two major types of strategy:

- Operational Strategy
- Transformational Strategy

Operational Strategy

Operational Strategy is the planning and accountable daily execution of the effective use of all the resources the business has.

Operational Strategy includes:

- Resource Management
- Waste Management
- Market Visibility
- Production/Sales Management
- Financial Management and Growth

Consistency in operational strategy helps the business successfully utilize its resources to achieve its transitions or hurdles on its Life Path or initiate strategies for recovery if needed.

The resources that will be developed are:

- Institutional Knowledge
- Competitive Product / Service
- Excellent Market Relationship Skills
- Committed Team and employable assets
- Passive Income and Healthy Capital Reserves

Operational Strategies is addressed in the *USB – Utility Solutions for Businesses by Cherry-Ann Craigwell.* In the next chapter we will address the various forms of transformational strategies that can be employed to assist the business on its life path journey.

Transformational Strategy

Transformational Strategy is the strategy that is periodically employed to guide the business through growth and development, transition stages and recovery.

The engagement of this strategy addresses actions like:

- Entering new markets
- Diversification
- Mergers and Acquisitions
- White Label Manufacturing / Subcontracting
- Franchising
- Start-up Plan
- Exit Plan

Transformational Strategy is a plan of action to introduce a change of operations that is necessary for when the business has to adjust its position in the market or to facilitate the natural life stages of the business.

This plan of action requires the business to identify with a purpose and consider the resources that are available to initiate action.

Strategy and Size

Being the right size and having the right strategy is important as the business will be able to use its resources effectively to adopt the best actions for its continued sustainability and development.

I will give an example of a transformational strategy implemented based on the resources of the business.

Example:

A Fast-Food Restaurant is owned by a young family with kids. The restaurant is doing quite well, as they have employed the 'family secret recipe' in their main course which attracts customers from very far. It has been expressed by their committed patrons to establish other outlets. The couple having to balance work / life commitments does not see this being viable for them to manage. A suggested strategy to employ here will be: Franchising.

Benefits of Franchising to the young family are:

- No capital output for the establishing of the additional outlet.
- Limited risks and liabilities.
- No increase in employee cost and employee management.
- Ability to reach a larger target market.
- Maintain customer brand loyalty.

A Franchise Agreement prepared in this situation will ensure the 'family secret recipe' is made available through the new franchised outlet that is more accessible to their patrons. This recipe can be prepared, by the young couple, packaged and delivered to the franchisee for use in the preparation of meals.

Accountability measures with penalties can be included in the Franchise Agreement to ensure standards are upheld.

An operational strategy that can be implemented is to enlist the restaurant on a Food Delivery App where their restaurant is in a network of delivery drivers that offer services of food delivery.

It will not be fitting for the young family at this time to invest in capital cost and management resources for their expansion, but also, it is not realistic for them to not capitalize on the favor the market has presented.

The implementation of a strategy at this juncture of the business is important to remain competitive in the market and help the business to successfully transition to its next stage in its life path.

Business Life Stages

The business like a living organism has to experience different stages from birth to death.

Some businesses die prematurely because not much effort is placed in understanding the different stages the business must experience.

Each stage of the business life brings new and different experiences and will require the business to implement strategies to adapt to the challenges and the expected growth of that stage.

The Business Life Stages/Cycle is a concept that has been developed in business management for many years and is used as a guide for growth and development strategies in businesses.

The following diagram highlights the underlying expectations of the different stages in the life path of a business.

ORGANIZATION LIFE STAGES

Success in achieving the expectations of a life stage supports the transition to the next.

TRUST

The first three years of an organization requires it to build trust in its network and customers. Strategies employed will be centered on monitoring, feedback and improvement.

SELF SUFFICIENCY

In its fourth year the organization should be generating a profit and reducing its liabilities. It is during this period capital generation and passive income strategies must be employed.

INNOVATION & ACTION

In its seventh year the organization can now comfortably employ transformational strategies. Its operational strategies should be institutionalized and effective, creating a stable backdrop for innovation and action on new products, new markets or new services.

ENTERPRISING

At its tenth year a strong operation with a stable network and new opportunities, the organization is in a place to settle and grow its sales and market presence.

DISTINCTION

The beginning of its fourteenth year the organization would have created its distinctive space in its market. Brand Loyalty and a strong Customer Relationship Management strategy will solidify this position.

COHESIVENESS

At its sixteenth year the organization is well poised in the market, it can comfortably engage in enhancing communication both internally and externally in the community. Community based Corporate Social Responsibility activities can be promoted.

COMMITMENT

The leaders, at the twentieth year of the organization, can evaluate its presence and the value it offers both internally and externally. Developing policies to ensure longevity for organization sustainability and market presence.

CONTINUITY

The habitual application of innovation and action, enterprising, distinction, cohesiveness and commitment allows the organization to create a strong market presence, sustainable network and employee loyalty making it a viable competitor in its industry

©Copyright 2021

Transitions of the business

Trust

Building trust is crucial to setting the right foundation for the business. It is important the business's interaction with its customers, employees and network is governed with integrity and meeting expectations. Monitoring, Feedback and Improvement are three key energies that must be exercised in this stage. If effectively done this stage should last for three years. Evidence of success will be in the significant reduction of start-up financial liabilities, a comfortable repeat customer base and a committed team.

Self Sufficiency

During this stage start-up financial liabilities must be completely cleared off and strategies concentrating on generating capital reserves and passive income must be employed. Institutional knowledge agreed on and implemented in daily accountable processes. Strategies on Business Process will be employed here. This is where the business begins to build its internal identity, a strong foundation of financial security and return customer base.

Innovation & Action

The business having gained trust and self-sufficiency and is now poised to initiate innovation and action. Innovation here is the consideration of creating a new product or entering into a new market (larger) that is, engaging in a Transformational Strategy. This is not increasing sale in an existing market or tweeting an existing product or service to an existing market. (Activities for existing products and existing markets are exercised daily in operational strategies). Some transformational strategies employed here will be Diversification, Mergers and Acquisitions or White Label Manufacturing / Sub Contracting.

Enterprising

In the enterprising stage the business can get down to working on increasing its market share with the existing products and services and the engaged transformational strategy employed from the previous stage of innovation and action. Operational Strategies for mass marketing, production and increasing sales should be effectively utilized at this stage. Transformational Strategies of Franchising and Exporting can be employed at this stage as well. This is the expansion stage.

Distinction

So, the business has expanded it is now to ensure that the products and services is distinctive in the market and against its competitors. Creating Brand Loyalty and distinction at this stage is recommended. Brand Loyalty strategies should be employed, through active customer relationship management in the markets that are more responsive to the business's products and services and rebranding.

Cohesiveness

The business exists in an eco-system and it is important that it maintains communication and interaction with the elements of its eco-system. These include the community, its suppliers, employees and shareholders. Strategies for creating business culture, internal brand loyalty and corporate social responsibility initiatives can be employed at this stage.

Commitment

The leaders can evaluate the presence and image the business has in the market and professional commitment from its team. They need to at this time review the business eco-system, ensuring the business has met its objectives and is resourced for its next phase.

The business owner ensures they have created the environment that has been intended for the business to be stable and well set for continuity.

Continuity

This phase of the business embraces the need to instill long term practices of habitual application of creativity, discipline, management practices, negotiating skills, networking, accountability measures and strategy that will realize the business longevity and success.

The business owner is encouraged to create a strong market presence and employee loyalty that is distinctive ensuring the business becomes a viable competitor in the industry.

Change is Constant

Your business is not spared from the reality of the continuity of change. The business exists in an environment that is fluid and responds to the behaviors of humans and the cycles of nature.

The Political, Economic, Social, Technological, Environmental and Legal elements of the industry supports an eco-system in which your business has to be sustained and developed.

It is expected that the elements can positively or negatively impact the business and it is important the business is in a position to adapt new thoughts and actions to navigate the changes for its continued existence.

The implementation of Transformational Strategy can be proactive or reactive. Most businesses that practice proactive transformational strategies tend to have a competitive advantage compared to those who are reactive to their environment.

Habitually improving on operational strategies and successfully completing the necessary steps at each of the business stages, the business will be poised to comfortably engage in transformational strategies

Transformational Strategy can be considered in three major elements of the business:-

Change in Governance

Change in governance considers the internal operations of the business. These include:

- Legal Structure
- Operations Structure
- Institutional Knowledge

Additional Product / Service

This is the addition of a new product / service to the business's operative revenue stream. The required research and development will have to be employed to ensure the viability of the new venture. An example will be a mini mart now providing fast food services.

Additional Target Market

A product / service may be created, normally, for a particular target market, but the business's products and services may also do well targeted to additional local and / or foreign markets.

All the above will require research and resources to be carried out effectively.

Transformational Strategy Components

A transformational strategy must have the following components.

Have a Goal

What is the objective to be achieved from this strategy?

- Change in legal structure to raise more financing?
- Develop and introduce a new product/service in the existing market?
- To enter foreign markets with existing product/service?

A Developed Plan

A developed plan answers questions such as:

Why does the business need a transformational strategy at this time? Is the business successful presently or is it failing in its operations?

What is the best strategy to engage in for the continuance of the business or the exit from the industry?

Who is the team that will be executing the transformational strategy?

How will the objective of the plan be achieved, that is; what are the processes to be implemented to ensure the plan is successful?

When, establishing the timelines to ensure control and accountability.

Executing Team

The team selected to execute the transformational strategy must be experienced, qualified and well networked to assist the business at this particular milestone. If necessary, contracting the right resource personnel should be an option.

Monitoring and Accountability

Transformational Strategy is best executed as a project. The elements of project management should be adopted ensuring completion and accountability of effective use of resources.

Process to Institutionalize

If the transformational strategy is done for the continuance of the business, the strategy completed must now be institutionalized into the business. If it is a new product/service, new target market or governance change, this must now be made aware and active in the operational strategies of the business, becoming institution knowledge.

Types of Transformational Strategies

Depending on the businesses operational strength and the environment Transformational strategies can be employed at key stages of the business. The following is a list and simple description of Transformational Strategies.

Start Up Strategy

The start-up strategy requires the 'to be business' to have a passion, resources and an operational plan to execute. A start-up strategy may take 2 – 3 years for a business to be successfully profitable.

Diversification

This is when the business changes its products and services. A farmer who traditionally cultivates pumpkins decides to rear livestock is an example of diversification.

Entering New Markets

Entering new markets can be done by either product enhancement for a new local market or original product for exports. Careful considerations must be made to the competition and substitutes that exists in the new market.

Franchising

Franchising is quite effective for the growth of fast food, retail and service businesses. This allows the brand of the particular business to be visible in the market while creating a larger consumer base.

White Label Manufacturing / Subcontracting

White Label Manufacturing / Sub Contracting create an opportunity for the business to offer its products / services without having to cover costs for market presentation. That includes costs for marketing, packaging and delivery.

Acquisitions

This can be an exit strategy for the business where another company has expressed interest in purchasing the book value of the business. The business must ensure that a valuation is done to ascertain the correct value of its operations.

The opposite can occur where the business can also acquire another company to increase its competitiveness and presence in the market and grow its customer base.

Mergers

A merger is the assimilation of two businesses for the purpose of building operation effectiveness, financial stability and larger market share.

Exit Plan

An exit plan should always be prepared once the business is operational. It includes how assets will be dispersed, customer relationships and employee termination managed.

There are two additional Transformational Strategies which will be covered in our chapter under Business Recovery. These are:

Business Impact Analysis

Business Continuity plan

The use of proactive transformational strategy in the business is particularly important as it helps the business to be proactive for growth, adjust to changes in the environment and comfortably supports the business through its transition stages.

Business Recovery

A business is not protected from the elements in the environment and may experience a disaster at any time. It is important therefore that consideration be given to proactively prepare a recovery process to minimize the negative effects, of a disaster if one does occur.

There are different types of disasters and for the purpose of this chapter we will scale them based on the impact they have on the business and its environment.

We must understand that a business exists in an eco-system consisting of local and foreign suppliers, local and foreign consumers, employees, legal bodies, financial bodies, business associations and competitors, and as such disasters that affects one or more elements of the ecosystem will affect the business.

A disaster can also happen from within the business, like a technology sabotage, where the damages is first felt by the business, but with the right business continuity plan the effects may not have to be felt by the business's ecosystem, such as its' customers and employees.

When a disaster occurs it is the business's responsibility to know;

- The minimum expected output that must be engaged to ensure survival to recovery and
- The operation that is necessary to facilitate survival mode.

Disaster preparedness will be different for the different types of disasters. As highlighted prior some disasters can be internal and some external to the business.

The understanding of what is required for survival mode of the business can be highlighted through the preparation of the Business Impact Analysis, and what process needs to be implemented is clarified in the Business Continuity Plan. Both of these will be addressed.

Types of Disasters

The different disasters can either be natural or man-made. Disasters can also happen to the business only or to any of the components in its eco-system. The following lists different disasters and they are scaled accordingly.

1. *Disasters that influence all elements in the eco-system of the business. (1)*
2. *Disasters that influence some elements of the eco-system of the business. (2)*
3. *Disaster that influences only the business. (3)*

Disaster	Scale
Employee Unrest	3
Robbery	3
Fire	3, 2
Flooding	3, 2
Technology Sabotage	1, 2, 3
Earthquake	2, 1
Tornadoes	2, 1
Hurricanes	2, 1
Volcanic Eruption	2, 1
Drought	2, 1
Political / Civil Unrest	2, 1
Disease / Virus Outbreaks	1

Category 3 listed disasters are scenarios that affect the business first and sometimes only the business. It is therefore proactive that the business includes in its operational strategy elements of occupational health and safety practices to minimize the risks of having a disaster happening in its operations.

Examples of occupational health and safety practice being part of the operational strategy are: the installation and maintenance of flood barriers on the premises, regular maintenance of fire extinguishers, external backup of company data, wearing of PPE, regular maintenance of camera systems and keeping insurance coverage current.

Category 2 and 1 are disasters that are caused due to external factors, national disasters. These disasters, the company cannot mitigate but can put measures in place to allow for business continuity, if one does occur.

When considering recovery, emphasis is placed on asset, resource and operation management recovery.

Assets of the business includes; plant and machinery, Furniture and Fixtures, Property, Inventory, Finances, Vehicles, Institutional Knowledge, Information and records.

The business's resources are its suppliers, communication channel, financial and business associations and employees.

The preparation of the Business Impact Analysis (BIA) and Business Continuity Plan (BCP) will help the business identify what resources will be affected, what operations will be impacted and the necessary solution to engage to ensure business continuity, depending on the disaster.

A simple table (Page 45) of a combined BIA /BCP guides the management on knowing what assets, resources and operations will be negatively affected and the best solutions to employ depending on the disaster experienced. This proactive approach will support the business in being able to respond immediately and objectively to any disaster.

Business Impact Analysis

As the term implies, the Business Impact Analysis, addresses what assets, resources and operations that will be affected in the event of a disaster. It considers an estimate loss of work time, value and customer satisfaction. It is also identifies what other supporting systems and network elements of the business that will be affected by any disaster.

Using the different categories as listed before the owner must identify what resources will be negatively affected based on the elements in each category.

Consideration must also be given to ensuring the values of the business at the time of the disaster is documented and confirmed, by having financial statements prepared timely and periodically.

This gives the business a comfortable idea as to what is the value of the business at the time of the disaster and guide insurers on a value that can be paid in compensation if losses are incurred.

Once the business is aware as to what resources can be negatively affected due to the different disasters, a business continuity plan must be developed to guarantee business continuity.

Business Continuity Plan

Business Continuity Plan is the termed coined for the strategy that has to be employed to ensure the business can function, at least at minimum output, during or immediately after a disaster.

The plan focuses on the customer and operations impact and what needs to be implemented to ensure the best possible operation that offers the least affected customer service.

Depending on the severity of customer impact and the customer relationship achieved in operations, an advisory may become necessary to inform your customers of the impact on service and the business's commitment on continued services and the capacity of such.

If an exit plan needs to be employed, a business valuation must be done based on the business's last financial statements, work in progress inventory, finished goods and raw materials. Liabilities should include the cost for disaster recovery efforts (if any).

Assets & Resources – Protection and Recovery

Adopting polices and processes for the protection and recovery of the business's assets must be a proactive undertaking by the business in all its ongoing contracts, negotiations and transactions.

In this chapter we will consider the different Assets & Resources of the business and the protection of such and if necessary, what recovery methods that can be applied to safeguard value.

Finance

All businesses exist to do one thing and that is to make a profit. It is important for the proper recording and analysis of your finances, which will determine whether your business is profitable or not. These must be accomplished through bookkeeping and financial statements, and the proper upkeep of bank records and financial investments. If possible quarterly internal paper filings should be kept for proof of financial position. Business insurance must also be kept current as your business can be covered for; General Liability, Commercial Property, Business Income, Worker's Compensation, Vehicle, Professional Liability and Data Breach.

The finance of the business gives an idea as to the value of the business at a given time. It is therefore important that one maintain current records so correct valuation can be ascertained in the time of a disaster.

Furniture & Fixtures

The furniture and fixtures of the business must be accounted for in a situation of a disaster. The value of all furniture and fixtures will be updated annually in an asset register. This register is an important part of your accounts and is updated with each asset purchase and its value. The value depreciates as per government guidelines for the recording of the devaluation of company's assets. The finance value or book value will be available from the updated or most current asset register.

Human Capital

The management of the human capital in a disaster is important as the business will have to determine which human resource is necessary for the recovery of the business. In the preparation of employee contracts / agreements and job description a clause must be included that specifically addresses disaster recovery and the components of the relationship between the business and the employee that will be affected.

Consideration should be given to hours of work, remuneration, responsibilities and termination.

Institution Knowledge

The business's institution knowledge has to be documented either or both electronically or hard copy. That is manuals, record keeping, processes, policies, customers' contracts, vendor and supplier relationships and contracts, legal papers, marketing material, accounts journals, accounts bookkeeping etc. The correct storage of these items means that they can be easily retrieved and be usable in the case of disaster where the company will be able to function to recovery.

Inventory

There are two types of inventory and these are; Finished Inventory and Work in Progress. It is important that the business keep a tally of its inventory daily as it supports analysis for cost vs. profits and states the value of products the business has presently. A disaster that affects the inventory of the business can be claimed under Business Income or Business Property Insurance.

Plant & Machinery

Plant and machinery are the required resources that produce the goods and services of the business. In a mini-mart plant and machinery will be its cash register, shelving and refrigeration. In a salon plant and machinery will be represented by the massage table or a hairdressers chair and unit.

Warranties and Manuals must be kept safely for all plant and machinery used in the business. This will be needed when a disaster occurs if information is required on operational use or for disposal.

Property

Commercial Property Insurance is available to ensure if there is damage to your building, you can have financial recourse to assist in the repairs of it. Precaution though must be exercised daily in the business operational strategies, to mitigate some disasters like flooding.

Raw Materials

Valuation of raw materials must be done simultaneously with the valuation of the business's inventory.

Vehicles

The current value of a vehicle will be recorded in the company's asset register and will reflect the depreciation value over a period of time. Also ensure the Insurance on the vehicles are current and properly registered. In the case of a disaster you will need to determine the need for the vehicles and if necessary sales value.

Opportunity in the Crisis

The Chinese symbol for crisis means *danger, a crucial point when something begins to change.*

As such in every crisis / disaster there is an opportunity, an opportunity to consider changes in policies, operations or products and services. Therefore, leveraging on the strengths of the business it allows the business to be innovative, and implement any of the necessary transformational strategies that were previously discussed to recover from a disaster.

Depending on the scale of the disaster that is, if the disaster affects the environment first, a national disaster, Levels 1 and 2 in our classification, the business will have support from national agencies and finance houses to facilitate business continuity.

Usually economic recovery after a national disaster may be at a lower base that is consumer buying power may decrease. In an environment where frugality has to be exercised the business should consider:

- Its cost of goods valuation;
- Diversifying to a fast-moving consumer good that is needed in the present market;
- Play it safe in balancing production to sales capacity and;

- Ensure the investment in diversifying is affordable.

Each national disaster leaves opportunities in specific industries. A business consideration should answer the following question: can I provide what the market needs and can afford for the business to comfortably recover from this disaster?

Diversification; Don't think it difficult to diversify if necessary, Samsung started its operations as a small trading company trading dried fish, local agriculture and noodles. Today they operate in electronics, construction and shipbuilding, to name a few, on a global level.

Business continuity for a Level 3 disaster, that is a disaster that influenced the business only, will be wholly dependent on the strengths and preparedness of the business.

It is wise to complete a plan to guide the necessary actions that should be undertaken by the business when any internal disaster occurs.

The following diagram gives an example as to what a simple plan in a table form can look like. With the proactive approach a business can ensure the necessary resources and operatives are in place to facilitate the successful implementation of 'survival mode'.

Business Impact Analysis / Business Continuity Plan

Disaster	Resource Affected	Operation Affected	Minimum Output	Action to Be taken
Employee Unrest	Human Resource	Sales Production	Sales—Standard sales volume to match minimum production capacity Production—Minimum production capacity as per machine or human output	Adjust purchase of raw material to match Production Commit to filling all sales order requests. Advise customers of any inconveniences That may occur Fill shortage of labor From pool of substitutes

Conclusion

In the preceding pages we looked at;

- Transition Strategies
- Transformational Strategies
- Recovery Strategies

These strategies are necessary to help the business accomplish continuity and growth.

They are unfortunately usually overlooked and not engaged proactively, while the business's existence is always supported with operations only and the market response.

The proactive approach in engaging the listed strategies allows the business to:

- Stay competitive in the market
- Maintain a stable financial position
- Experience stable and continuous growth
- Develop a cohesive and strong stakeholder network
- Have external and internal Brand Loyalty
- Sustainable recovery operations

As a business owner, the importance of success in your venture is important for yourself first, employees, customers, suppliers and network.

Engaging in the listed strategies will require your commitment (discipline) and inspiration so as to ensure your venture is successful.

The business journey can be adopted by anyone and embracing the right knowledge and energy the business will realize the success of profitability, stability and longevity.

www.ingramcontent.com/pod-product-compliance
Lightning Source LLC
Chambersburg PA
CBHW041942240526
45473CB00033B/393